MOCKTAILS
100 RECIPES

CTC Editore

© **Copyright 2022 by ____CTC EDITORE_____**

All rights reserved.

This document is geared towards providing exact and reliable information with regards to the topic and issue covered. The publication is sold with the idea that the publisher is not required to render accounting, officially permitted, or otherwise, qualified services. If advice is necessary, legal or professional, a practiced individual in the profession should be ordered.

- From a Declaration of Principles which was accepted and approved equally by a Committee of the American Bar Association and a Committee of Publishers and Associations.

In no way is it legal to reproduce, duplicate, or transmit any part of this document in either electronic means or in printed format. Recording of this publication is strictly prohibited and any storage of this document is not allowed unless with written permission from the publisher. All rights reserved.

The information provided herein is stated to be truthful and consistent, in that any liability, in terms of inattention or otherwise, by any usage or abuse of any policies, processes, or directions contained within is the solitary and utter responsibility of the recipient reader. Under no circumstances will any legal responsibility or blame be held against the publisher for any reparation, damages, or monetary loss due to the information herein, either directly or indirectly.

Respective authors own all copyrights not held by the publisher.

The information herein is offered for informational purposes solely, and is universal as so. The presentation of the information is without contract or any type of guarantee assurance.

The trademarks that are used are without any consent, and the publication of the trademark is without permission or backing by the trademark owner. All trademarks and brands within this book are for clarifying purposes only and are the owned by the owners themselves, not affiliated with this document

Contents

Important! 7
Pink Melon 8
PPC 8
Citrus Power 9
Watermelon julep 9
Sweet and Spicy 10
Shirley Temple 10
Color Madness 11
Old Brew Tonic 11
Blueberry mess 12
Flower Power 12
Nospresso Martini 13
Green Gains 43
Kiwi Martini 14
Virgin Bellini 14
Virgin Paloma 15
Blackberry Fusion 15
Arnold Palmer 16
Virgin Mary 16
Pinky Tale 17
Hibiscus temptation 17
Lime Rickey 18
Cinderella 18
Strawberry basil smash 19
Fake Americano 19
Orange Raspberry 20
Melon Cream 20
Green essentials 21
Lavender Collins 21
Sunset Lover 22
Matcha Latte 22
Coffee sour 23
Lemon Rickey 23
1 oz Lemon Juice 23
Lychee Mandarin Mocktail 24
Kiwi Express 24

Virgin French 75	25
Pineapple Sour	25
Minty Blackberry	26
Butterfly and ginger	26
Crystal Flower	27
Virgin Spritz	27
Apple Tonic	28
Virgin Mojito	28
PiNOcolada	29
Raspberry Basil Mojito	29
Pumpkin Daiquiri	30
Green Garden	30
LML	31
Espresso Tonic	31
Basil Cherry	32
Lemon Soda	32
Virgin Hurricane	33
Fake Spritz	33
Virgin Mai Tai	34
Apple highball	34
Primary color	35
Kiwi Mojito	35
Purple Dream	36
Shot of Health	36
Are you liking the book?	37
Strawberry Matcha Latte	38
Chocolate Sunset	38
Power Gain	39
Tropical Blu	39
Grapefruit Spritz	40
Virgin San Francisco	40
Amaretto Sour	41
Cherry Bit	41
Virgin G & T	42
Coffee Mojito	42
Cucumber Mint smash	43
Orange Rosemary	13

Florida 44

Watermelon Lime 44

Virgin Rossini 45

Blueberry Mojito 45

Blueberry Sky 46

Orange Moscow Mule 46

Banana Cream 47

Virgin Cosmopolitan 47

Buffalo Bill 48

Pink Lemonade 48

Virgin Strawberry Daiquiri 49

Virgin Blu Lagoon 49

Spicy Grapefruit 50

Virgin Tequila sunrise 50

Lime Soda 51

Pregnant Cocktail 51

Mango Time 52

Afterglow 52

Pineapple Orange 53

Red Lavender 53

Virgin Margarita 54

No Alcohol Appletini 54

Non Alcoholic Sangria 55

Pricklyberry 56

Virgin Mimosa 56

Blueberry Fusion 57

Atomic Orange 57

Blackberry Julep 58

9 Buche 58

Important!

We recommend the use fresh juices when possible. Bottled juice will reduce the quality and flavors of the drinks, making them less enjoyable.

Pink Melon

2 oz Seedlip grove 42

⅔ oz Melon Syrup

⅔ oz Ruby Red Grapefruit Juice

Egg White or Aquafaba

Method: Add all the ingredients in a shaker and shake for about 10 seconds. Add the ice and shake for another 10 seconds. Strain into a champagne glass.

No garnish required

PPC

½ Mango

1 oz Pineapple juice

1 oz Carrot juice

0.5 oz Passion fruit syrup

Method: Add all the ingrendients in a blender with a cup of ice and blend. Pour into a glass.

Garnish: Edible flower.

Citrus Power

1 oz Lemon Juice

1 oz Lime Juice

1 oz Orange Juice

1 oz Mandarin Juice

1 oz Agave Syrup

Method: Add all the ingredients in a shaker with ice and shake for about 10 seconds. Strain into an old-fashioned glass filled with ice.

Garnish: Orange slice

Watermelon julep

5-6 chunks of Watermelon

6 Mint Leaves

1 oz Lemon Juice

¼ oz Simple Syrup

3 oz Elderflower Tonic Water

Method: add all the ingredients except the tonic water in a julep glass and muddle them., then add some ice and the tonic water.

Garnish: Watermelon slice.

Sweet and Spicy

1.5 oz Prickly Pear Juice

½ oz Lemon Juice

3 oz Ginger Beer

Method: Add all the ingredients except the ginger ale in a shaker with ice and shake for about 10 seconds. Strain in a tall glass filled with ice and add the ginger beer.

Garnish: Lemon slice

Shirley Temple

½ oz Grenadine Syrup

4 oz Ginger Ale

Method: Pour the ingredients in a champagne glass filled with crushed ice and lightly stir.

Garnish: Maraschino cherry.

Color Madness

1 oz Cold Butterfly Pea Tea

½ oz Lime Juice

3 oz Tonic Water

Method: Add all the ingredients in a highball glass filled with ice and lightly stir.

Garnish: Orange slice.

Old Brew Tonic

2 oz Cold Brew Coffee

5 oz Tonic Water

Method: Add all the ingredients in a highball glass filled with ice and lightly stir.

No garnish required

Blueberry mess

8 Blueberries

6-8 Mint Leaves

1 Teaspoon of Sugar

½ oz Lime Juice

Sprite to top

Method: In an old-fashioned glass, muddle the blueberries with the sugar and the lime juice, add the mint, the ice and the sprite and lightly stir.

Garnish: Mint sprig.

Flower Power

1.5 oz Chamomile

3 oz Orange Juice

Method: Pour the ingredients in a champagne glass filled with crushed ice and lightly stir.

Garnish: Orange slice.

Nospresso Martini

1 Espresso

2 oz Coffee Milk

Method: Add all the ingredients in a shaker with ice and shake for about 10 seconds, then strain in a cocktail glass.

Garnish: Coffee beans.

Orange Rosemary

1 ½ oz Orange Juice

½ oz Grenadine Syrup

3 oz Soda water

Rosemary Sprig

Method: Add all the ingredients in a highball glass filled with ice and lightly stir.

Garnish: Rosemary.

Kiwi Martini

1.5 oz NA Gin

1 oz Kiwi Juice

½ oz Orange Juice

½ oz Ginger Syrup

½ oz Lime Juice

Method: Add all the ingredients in a shaker with ice and shake for about 10 seconds. Strain into a martini glass.

Garnish: Kiwi slice

Virgin Bellini

1 oz Peach Puree

3 oz Soda Water

Method: Pour the ingredients in a cocktail glass and stir until the puree is dissolved.

Garnish: Edible flower

Virgin Paloma

⅔ oz Agave Nectar

½ oz Lime Juice

1.5 oz Grapefruit Juice

1.5 oz Soda Water

Method: Add all the ingredients in a highball glass and lightly stir.

Garnish: Grapefruit slice.

Blackberry Fusion

5 Blackberries

3 oz Soda Water

Method: Muddle the blackberries in an old-fashioned glass filled with ice, then add the soda

Garnish: Blackberries, mint, and a lemon twist

Arnold Palmer

4 oz Iced Tea

2 oz Lemonade

Method: Add all the ingredients in a highball glass filled with ice and lightly stir.

Garnish: Lemon slice.

Virgin Mary

3 oz Tomato juice

½ oz lemon juice

Few drops of Tabasco

Few drops of Worcestershire sauce

A pinch of salt and pepper

Method: Add all the ingredients in a highball glass filled with ice and lightly stir.

Garnish: Celery stick or lemon slice.

Pinky Tale

1.5 oz Strawberry puree

½ oz Lychee puree

½ oz lemon juice

¼ oz Simple Syrup

3 oz Ginger Ale

Method: Add all the ingredients but the ginger ale in a shaker with ice and shake for about 10 seconds.. Strain into a highball glass filled with ice and top it with the ginger ale.

Garnish: Strawberry

Hibiscus temptation

2 oz Hibiscus Tea

1 oz Lime Juice

½ oz Simple Syrup

3 oz Ginger Beer

Method: Add all the ingredients in a highball glass filled with ice and lightly stir.

Garnish: Lime wheel.

Lime Rickey

1 oz Lime Juice

½ oz Simple Syrup

3 oz Soda Water

Method: Add all the ingredients in a highball glass filled with ice and lightly stir.

Garnish: Lime slice.

Cinderella

1 oz Orange Juice

1 oz Lemon Juice

1 oz Pineapple Juice

⅓ oz Grenadine Syrup

Ginger Ale to top

Method: Add all the ingredients but the ginger ale in a shaker with ice and shake for about 10 seconds. then strain into a highball glass and fill with the ginger ale.

Garnish: Pineapple slice.

Strawberry basil smash

1.5 oz NA gin

4 Strawberries

6 Basil Leaves

¾ oz Lemon Juice

½ oz Simple Syrup

Method: add all the ingredients in a shaker and muddle them. then add the ice and shake for 10 seconds. Strain into a coupe glass.

Garnish: Strawberry and basil leaf .

Fake Americano

1.5 oz San Bitter

1.5 oz Chinotto

Method: Add all the ingredients in an old-fashioned glass filled with ice and lightly stir Garnish: Orange slice and double twist of lemon.

Garnish: Lemon twist and orange slice.

Orange Raspberry

⅔ oz Raspberry Syrup

⅓ oz Lemon Juice

4 oz Orange Juice

Method: Add all the ingredients in a shaker with ice and shake for about 10 seconds. Strain into a highball glass filled with ice.

Garnish: Orange slice.

Melon Cream

150 grams of Melon

1 ½ scoop of Vanilla Ice Cream

4 oz Milk

Method: Add all the ingredients in a blender and blend. Pour into a tall glass.

Garnish: Melon slice.

Green essentials

4 oz Spinach Juice

4 oz Cucumber

1 Green Apple

4 oz Pineapple Juice

Method: Add all the ingredients with a cup of ice and blend. Pour into a tall glass.

No garnish required.

Lavender Collins

1 oz Lemon Juice

½ oz Lavender Syrup

4 oz Tonic Water

Method: Add all the ingredients in a highball glass filled with ice and lightly stir.

Garnish: Lemon slice.

Sunset Lover

1.5 oz Strawberry Puree

⅔ oz Lychee Puree

3 oz Tonic Water

Method: Add the purees in a shaker with ice and shake for about 10 seconds. Strain into a highball glass filled with ice and add the tonic water.

Garnish: Strawberries.

Matcha Latte

1 tsp Matcha

4 oz Hot Milk

Method: Pour in a cup the hot milk and the matcha, stir until combined.

Garnish: matcha powder.

Coffee sour

2 oz Cold Brew

1 oz Lemon Juice

½ oz Simple Syrup

Method: Add all the ingredients in a shaker with ice and shake for about 10 seconds. Strain into an old-fashioned glass filled with ice.

Garnish: Lemon wedge.

Lemon Rickey

1 oz Lemon Juice

½ oz Simple Syrup

3 oz Soda Water

Method: Add all the ingredients in a highball glass filled with ice and lightly stir.

Garnish: Lemon slice.

Lychee Mandarin Mocktail

1 oz Lychee Puree

1.5 oz Mandarin Juice

3 oz Ginger Ale

Method: Add the puree and the juice in a shaker with ice and shake for about 10 seconds. Strain into a highball glass filled with ice and add the ginger ale.

Garnish: Mandarin slice.

Kiwi Express

1 Kiwi

1.5 oz Black Tea

¾ oz Elderflower Syrup

4 oz Sprite

Method: Blend the Kiwi with the tea, the syrup, and a cup of ice. Pour in a tall glass and top it up with sprite.

Garnish: Kiwi wheel.

Virgin French 75

1.5 oz Lemon Juice

4 oz Tonic Water

Method: Add the ingredients in a champagne glass and ligjtly stir.

Garnish: Lemon twist.

Pineapple Sour

2 oz Pineapple Juice

1 oz Lemon Juice

½ oz Strawberry Syrup

1 tsp Rose Water

Egg White or Aquafaba

Method: Add all the ingredients in a shaker with ice and shake for about 10 seconds. Strain into a coupe glass.

Garnish: Pineapple slice.

Minty Blackberry

6 Mint Leaves

4 Blackberries

½ oz Mint Syrup

3 oz Sprite

Method: Add in a highball glass. the mint, the mint syrup, and the blackberries and muddle them. Add some ice and the sprite.

Garnish: Lime wheel and a blackberry.

Butterfly and ginger

1.5 oz Butterfly Pea Tea

½ oz Lemon Juice

3 oz Ginger Beer

Method: Add all the ingredients in a highball glass filled with ice and lightly stir.

Garnish: Edible flower.

Crystal Flower

1 oz Elderflower Syrup

⅓ oz Lemon Juice

4 oz Soda Water

Method: Add all the ingredients in a highball glass filled with ice and lightly stir.

Garnish: Lemon slice and mint sprig.

Virgin Spritz

1.5 oz San Bitter

½ oz Orange juice

3 oz Tonic Water

Method: Add all the ingredients in a wine glass filled with ice and lightly stir.

Garnish: Orange slice.

Apple Tonic

2 oz Apple juice

½ oz lime juice

½ oz Ginger syrup

3 oz Tonic Water

Method: Add all the ingredients but the tonic water in a shaker with ice and shake for about 10 seconds. Strain into a highball glass filled with ice and top it with the tonic water.

Garnish: Apple slices.

Virgin Mojito

8 Mint leaves

2 teaspoons of Sugar

¾ oz Lime Juice

Soda Water to top

Method: Add all the ingredients in a highball glass filled with ice and lightly stir.

Garnish: Mint sprig

PiNOcolada

3 oz Pineapple juice

2 oz Heavy cream

1 oz Coconut cream

Method: Add all the ingredients in a shaker with ice and shake for about 10 seconds. Strain into an old-fashioned glass filled with ice.

Garnish: Pineapple leaves.

Raspberry Basil Mojito

3 Raspberries

6-8 Basil Leaves

1 oz Lime Juice

2 Bar spoon of granulated sugar

1 ½ oz Ginger Ale

Method: In a highabll glass, muddle the raspberries with the sugar, the basil and the lime juice. Add some ice and the ginger ale and lightly stir.

Garnish: Raspberry and basil leaves.

Pumpkin Daiquiri

1 oz Ronsin (non alcoholic rum)

1 oz Pumpkin puree

1 oz Cinnamon and nutmeg syrup

½ oz Lime juice

½ oz Egg white or Aquafaba

Syrup: add the spices to a simple syrup and let infuse for a few hours.

Method: Add all the ingredients in a shaker with ice and shake for about 10 seconds. Strain into a cocktail glass.

Garnish: Cinnamon stick and gratulated nutmeg.

Green Garden

1.5 oz Seedlip Garden 108

¼ oz Basil Syrup

3 oz Tonic Water

Method: Add all the ingredients in an old-fashioned glass filled with ice and lightly stir.

Garnish: Basil leaf

LML

1 oz Lime Juice

1 oz Lemon Juice

½ oz Simple Syrup

6-8 Mint Sprig

3 Soda Water

Method: Pour all the ingredients in a shaker filled with ice except the soda and shake for 10 seconds, fine strain into a tall glass filled with ice and add the soda.

Garnish: Lemon or lime wheel.

Espresso Tonic

1 Espresso

4 oz Tonic Water

Method: Add all the ingredients in a highball glass filled with ice and lightly stir..

Garnish: Lemon slice .

Basil Cherry

1.5 oz Cherry Puree

¾ oz Lemon Juice

½ oz Basil Syrup

2 oz Chinotto

Method: Add all the ingredients but the chinotto in a shaker with ice and shake for about 10 seconds. Strain into a highball glass filled with ice and top it with the tonic water.

Garnish: Maraschino cherry

Lemon Soda

1 oz Lemon juice

1 oz Simple syrup

3 oz Soda water

Method: Add all the ingredients in a highball glass filled with ice and lightly stir.

Garnish: Lemon wedge.

Virgin Hurricane

2 oz Orange juice

2 oz Cranberry juice

1 oz Grapefruit Juice

1 oz Apple Juice

Method: Add all the ingredients in a shaker with ice and shake for about 10 seconds. Strain into a highball glass filled with ice.

Garnish: Orange slice.

Fake Spritz

1.5 oz Crodino

½ oz Orange juice

3 oz Tonic Water

Method: Pour the ingredients in a wine glass filled with ice and stir.

Garnish: Orange slice

Virgin Mai Tai

1 ½ oz Orange juice

½ oz Almond syrup

¾ oz Lime juice

½ oz simple syrup

Method: Add all the ingredients in a shaker with ice and shake for about 10 seconds. Strain into an old-fashioned glass filled with crushed ice.

Garnish: Maraschino cherry.

Apple highball

1 ½ Zero proof Whiskey

1 oz Apple juice

3 oz Ginger beer

Method: Add all the ingredients in a highball glass filled with ice and lightly stir.

Garnish: Apple slices.

Primary color

4 oz Orange Juice

1 oz Blue Curaçao Syrup

½ oz Lemon Juice

Method: Add all the ingredients in a shaker with ice and shake for about 10 seconds. Strain into a highball glass filled with ice

Garnish: Orange slice.

Kiwi Mojito

1 Kiwi

1 oz Lime Juice

1 oz Honey Syrup

2 oz Sprite

Method: Cut the kiwi into pieces, then in a highball glass, muddle the kiwi with the honey and the lime juice. Add some ice and the sprite and lightly stir.

Garnish: Strawberry and basil leaves.

Purple Dream

1 oz NA Vodka

2-3 chunks of red Pitaya

4 oz Sprite

Method: In a highabll glass, muddle the pitaya, then add some ice, the non alcoholic vodka and the sprite and lightly stir.

Garnish: Pitaya slice.

Shot of Health

1 oz Kiwi Juice

1 oz Carrot Juice

½ oz Ginger Juice

½ oz Lime Juice

Method: Add all the ingredients in a shaker with ice and shake for about 10 seconds. Strain into a shot glass.

No garnish required.

Are you liking the book?
This is who we are!

Scan the QR code to check us out on Instagram and discover more recipes, pictures, and facts about bartending!

Please let us know if there is anything we can do to improve our book or if you have any questions.

Strawberry Matcha Latte

4 chopped Strawberries

1 teaspoon of Matcha Powder

1 cup of water

3 oz Milk

Method: First bring the cup of water to boil and mixed with the matcha powder. Then place the strawberries at the bottom of a tall glass, then add some ice, the milk, and lastly pour 1 ½ oz of the matcha.

No garnish required.

Chocolate Sunset

4 oz Coconut Milk

1 cup of Chocolate Ice Cream

Method: Add all the ingredients in a blender and blend. Pour into a glass.

Garnish: Gratulated chocolate.

Power Gain

2 oz Spinach juice

½ Banana

5 oz Soy Milk

Method Add all the ingredients in a blender with a cup of ice and blend. Pour into a glass.

Garnish: Spinach leaf.

Tropical Blu

1 ½ oz Pineapple Juice

¾ oz Blu Curaçao Syrup

½ oz Lemon Juice

3 oz Coconut Cream

Method: Add all the ingredients in a shaker with ice and shake for about 10 seconds. Strain into an old-fashioned glass filled with ice.

Garnish: Maraschino cherry and pineapple wedge

Grapefruit Spritz

1 ½ oz Ruby Red Grapefruit Juice

½ oz Honey Syrup

3 oz Tonic Water

Method: Add all the ingredients in a highball glass filled with ice and lightly stir.

Garnish: Grapefruit slice.

Virgin San Francisco

2 ½ oz Orange Juice

1 oz Pineapple Juice

1 oz Orange Juice

¾ oz Grenadine Syrup

Method: Add all the ingredients in a shaker with ice and shake for about 10 seconds. Strain into a highball glass filled with ice and slowly pour the grenadine.

Garnish: Pineapple wedge.

Amaretto Sour

2 oz Pineapple Juice

¾ oz Lemon Juice

¼ oz Orgeat

¼ oz Maraschino Cherry Syrup

Method: Add all the ingredients in a shaker with ice and shake for about 10 seconds. Strain into an old-fashioned glass filled with ice

Garnish: Maraschino cherry and pineapple wedge.

Cherry Bit

½ Banana

2 oz Cherry puree

1 oz Beetroot Juice

2 oz Almond Milk

Method: Add all the ingredients in a blender with a cup of ice and blend. Pour into a glass.

No garnish required.

Virgin G & T

1.5 oz NA Gin

4 oz Tonic Water

Method: Add all the ingredients in a highball glass filled with ice and lightly stir.

Garnish: Lemon slice.

Coffee Mojito

1 Espresso

½ oz Mint Syrup

2 oz Soda Water

6-8 Mint Leaves

Method: Shake the espresso with ice until chilled, then pour it into a tall glass. Add the mint leaves, the syrup and some ice and lightly stir. Then add the soda.

Garnish: Mint Sprig.

Cucumber Mint smash

¼ of Cucumber

10 mint leaves

½ oz Lime Juice

½ oz Simple Syrup

1 ½ oz Ginger ale

Method: Blend all the ingredients with 3 to 4 ice cubes except the ginger ale, then pour into a tall glass and add the ginger ale.

Garnish: Lime wheel and mint leaves.

Green Gains

3 oz Milk

½ Avocado

Method: Blend the avocado and the milk, then Pour into a water glass.

No garnish required.

Florida

2 oz Grapefruit Juice

1 oz Orange Juice

¾ oz Lemon Juice

½ oz Grenadine Syrup

Tonic water to top

Method: First pour the grenadine at the bottom of a tall glass filled with ice.

Pour the juices in a shaker filled with ice and shake for 10 seconds, strain into the tall glass, add the tonic water and lightly stir.

Garnish: Orange slice.

Watermelon Lime

3 Cups of frozen diced Watermelon

1 oz Lime Juice

Method: Blend all the ingredients with some ice cubes and pour into a tall glass.

Garnish: Watermelon Slice.

Virgin Rossini

1 oz Strawberry puree

3 oz Soda Water

Method: Add the ingredients in a cocktail glass and stir until the puree is dissolved.

Garnish: Strawberry

Blueberry Mojito

6-8 Blueberries

6-8 Mint Leaves

1 Teaspoon of Sugar

¾ oz Lime Juice

Sprite to top

Method: In a highball glass, muddle the blueberries, then add the mint, the sugar and the lime juice and stir. Add some ice and the sprite and lightly stir.

Garnish: Mint Sprig.

Blueberry Sky

2 oz Blueberry Puree

1 oz Lemon Juice

½ oz Vanilla Syrup

1 oz Ginger Beer

Method: Add all the ingredients but the ginger beer in a shaker with ice and shake for about 10 seconds, strain into an old fashioned glass filled with ice and add the ginger beer.

Garnish: Blueberries.

Orange Moscow Mule

2 oz Orange Juice

½ oz Lime Juice

4 oz Ginger Beer

Method: Add all the ingredients in a julep mug filled with ice and lightly stir.

Garnish: Mint Sprig.

Banana Cream

½ Banana

1 cup of Vanilla Ice Cream

3 oz Milk

Method: Add all the ingredients in a blender with a cup of ice and blend. Pour into a glass.

Garnish: Banana slice.

Virgin Cosmopolitan

3 oz Cranberry Juice

1 oz Lime Juice

1 oz Orange Juice

¼ oz Simple Syrup

Method: Add all the ingredients in a shaker with ice and shake for about 10 seconds. Strain into a coupe glass.

Garnish: Orange twist.

Buffalo Bill

3 oz Orange juice

¾ oz Grenadine syrup

1 Egg yolk

Method: Add all the ingredients in a shaker with ice and shake for about 10 seconds. Strain into a coupe glass.

Garnish: Orange slice.

Pink Lemonade

4 raspberries

1 oz Lemon Juice

½ oz Simple Syrup

3 oz Sprite

Method: : In a highball glass, muddle the raspberries, then add ice and the other ingredients and lightly stir.

Garnish: Lemon slice.

Virgin Strawberry Daiquiri

4 Strawberries

⅔ oz Simple Syrup

1 oz Lime Juice

3 oz Sprite

Method: Add all the ingredients in a blender with a cup of ice and blend. Pour into a cocktail glass.

Garnish: Strawberry.

Virgin Blu Lagoon

1 oz Lemon Juice

¾ oz Blu Curaçao Syrup

4 oz Sprite

Method: Add all the ingredients in a highball glass filled with ice and lightly stir.

Garnish: Lemon slice.

Spicy Grapefruit

3 oz Grapefruit Juice

½ oz Lime Juice

1 to 3 slice of Jalapeño

6-8 Mint leaves

4 oz Ginger Beer

Method: Put the Jalapeño, the lime and the grapefruit in a shaker and muddle them. Add the mint and stir to combine the ingredients. Shake with ice for about 10 second and pour in a tall glass filled with ice before adding the ginger beer.

Garnish: Grapefruit slice.

Virgin Tequila sunrise

6 oz Orange juice

1 oz Grenadine Syrup

Method: Fill a highball glass with ice and pour the orange juice, then slowly pour the grenadine syrup.

Garnish: Orange slice.

Lime Soda

1 oz Lime juice

1 oz Simple syrup

3 oz Soda water

Method: Add all the ingredients in a highball glass filled with ice and lightly stir.

Garnish: Lime wedge.

Pregnant Cocktail

1 oz Apple Juice

1 oz Cranberry Juice

1 oz Orange Juice

½ oz Lemon Juice

½ oz Simple Syrup

Method: Add all the ingredients in a shaker with ice and shake for about 10 seconds, strain into an old fashioned glass filled with ice.

Garnish: Orange slice.

Mango Time

1 oz Mango Puree

1 ½ oz Orange Juice

4 oz Ginger Beer

Method: Add all the ingredients in a highball glass filled with ice and lightly stir..

Garnish: Mint Sprig.

Afterglow

1 ½ oz Pineapple juice

1 ½ oz Orange juice

¾ oz Grenadine syrup

Method: Add all the ingredients in a shaker with ice and shake for about 10 seconds. Strain into a coupe glass.

Garnish: Orange slice.

Pineapple Orange

1 ½ oz Orange Juice

1 ½ oz Pineapple Juice

4 oz Ginger Ale

Method: Add all the ingredients in a highball glass filled with ice and lightly stir.

Garnish: Pineapple Wedge.

Red Lavender

1 oz Lemon Juice

½ oz Lavender Syrup

¼ oz Grenadine Syrup

1 oz Soda Water

Method: Add all the ingredients except the soda in a shaker with ice and shake for about 10 seconds. Strain into an old fashioned glass filled with ice and add the soda.

Garnish: Lemon slice.

Virgin Margarita

2 oz Agave

1 oz lime juice

½ oz Grapefruit juice

½ oz Simple Syrup

2 Drops Orange Blossom Water

½ Teaspoon Chily Powder

Method: Add all the ingredients in a blender with a cup of ice and blend. Pour into a cocktail glass.

Garnish: Lime wheel.

No Alcohol Appletini

1 ½ oz Apple Juice

1 oz Lemon Juice

1 oz Green Apple Syrup

Method: Add all the ingredients in a shaker with ice and shake for about 10 seconds. Strain into a coupe glass.

Garnish: Apple slices.

Non Alcoholic Sangria

2 Cups of Cranberry Juice

2 Cups of Grape Juice

1 Cup of Orange Juice

½ Cup of Lemon Juice

4 Cups of Sparkling Water (or Sprite)

2 sliced lemon

2 sliced lime

1 sliced orange

1 sliced apple

4 sliced strawberries

Method: Pour all the ingredients into a large Pitcher and stir. Store it in the fridge before serving.

No garnish required.

Pricklyberry

1 oz Prickly Pear puree

1 oz Blueberry puree

½ oz lemon juice

¼ oz Simple Syrup

3 oz Tonic Water

Method: Add all the ingredients except the tonic water in a shaker with ice and shake for about 10 seconds. Strain into an old fashioned glass filled with ice and add the tonic water.

Garnish: Blueberries.

Virgin Mimosa

2 oz Orange Juice

4 oz Sprite

Method: Add all the ingredients in a champagne glass and lightly stir.

Garnish: Orange slice.

Blueberry Fusion

6 Blueberries

½ oz Lime juice

½ oz simple Syrup

3 oz Soda Water

Method: In a highabll glass, muddle the blueberries with the syrup, l and the lime juice. Add some ice and the soda and lightly stir.

Garnish: Blueberry and a lime wheel.

Atomic Orange

1 ½ oz Orange juice

3 oz Tonic water

Method: Add all the ingredients in a highball glass filled with ice and lightly stir.

Garnish: Orange slice.

Blackberry Julep

3 Blackberries

6-8 Mint Leaves

¾ oz Lime Juice

½ oz Simple Syrup

Soda Water to top

Method: In a highball glass, muddle the blackberries, then add the mint, the sugar and the lime juice and stir. Add some ice, top with the soda and lightly stir.

Garnish: Blackberry and mint sprig.

9 Buche

1.5 oz San Bitter

1.5 oz Bitter Orange Soda

Method: Add all the ingredients in a wine glass filled with ice and lightly stir.

Garnish: Orange slice.

Printed in Great Britain
by Amazon